shapes

Written by Monica Hughes

Collins

A square.

A triangle.

5

A circle.

A rectangle.

9

A star.

A hexagon.

13

Shapes

square

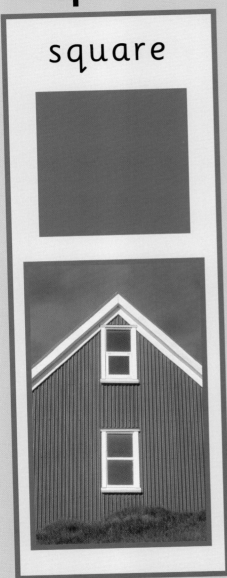

triangle

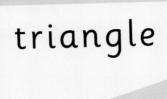

circle

rectangle

star

hexagon

Ideas for reading

Written by Kelley Taylor
Educational Consultant

Reading objectives:
- read and understand simple sentences
- demonstrate understanding when talking with others about what they have read
- read some common irregular words

Communication and language objectives:
- listen attentively in a range of situations
- express themselves effectively, showing awareness of listeners' needs
- follow instructions involving several ideas or actions
- answer "why" questions in response to stories or events

Curriculum links: Mathematical Development;

Numeracy: Shape and Space; Art & Design

High frequency word: a

Interest words: square, triangle, circle, rectangle, star, hexagon, shapes

Word count: 12

Resources: small whiteboard and pen, magazines

Build a context for reading

- Explain that we can find shapes all around us, and this book gives clues about where to look.

- Draw a square on the whiteboard and ask the children to look for one in the classroom. Repeat with a circle.

- Read the title and ask the children to name the shapes they see on the front cover. Emphasise the terms *title* and *cover*.

- Show the children how to turn to the title page. Ask them to say what shape they see. *Where does it tell me who wrote the book?* Explain that this is the author's name.

- Walk through the book looking at the shape on each left-hand page, finding it on the right-hand page.

Understand and apply reading strategies

- Ask the children to whisper to a partner the kind of shape they see on p2. Ask them to read the words to themselves and point as they go.